IF ...
COULD FIND
HER BEAUTY
OF CREATIVITY
THEN KINDNESS
WOULD SURELY
FIND HER HOME

Musings Of A Madman

Musings Of A Madman

Nathaniel Papahawk Goldberg

To order additional copies of this book, contact:
Xlibris Corporation
1-888-795-4274
www.Xlibris.com
Orders@Xlibris.com
80084

CONTENTS

Looking For Madonna 9
Chaos and Kisses 10
Out in Zipaquira 12
A Hand in the Dark 14
Dancing Huevos...16
In the park with A. 18
A touch of Summer White 19
Is it an Illusion? 21
Loretta's Limo..23
Across the Night time sadness 24
Big Mistake..25
A Strangest Day 28
One Station Plaza...30
Funny You Should Say That 32

CASSANDRA

A Touch of Summer in Winter 37
Cassandra doing Washington Square again.................................... 40
Cassandra's Beauty Beneath..41
Cassandra in the Rain 43
Cassandra—Chapter two...44
Cassandra at Smalls 45
Cassandra's Moon at Croton 47
A Day Well Spent 03-11-04 48
I Haven't Forgotten 49
In The Night 51
No weeping willows in C Park..52
My Father Is 54
Senasqua..56
What love tastes of 57

Summer Snow 58
A Tree'less Orchid 60
A Bottle Of Wine 63
Finding You 64
Shakespeare and Co. 66
Village Underground 70
A Bare Room 71
Around The Rainbow—Jazz Po 06-17-01 Dr. Hawk 73
A Wind Chilled Day In New York 74
A Night to Her 75
But Pure Infinity 77
The Night Before 78
What I need most 79

ADRIANA

Adriana's Magic 83
The pain of death within 84
A Walk with My Lady 85
Next To My Lady 87
I'm Not With Her Now 88
You and Me at the A and P 90
You Balance My Lopsided World 92
Deja Vous..93
Ginsberg 94
Metro Politan Madness 97
Paris You're Jewish 99
The Music Gone...101
September In Paris..103
What actually killed Papa? 07-16-08 104
Ode To A Shell 106
A Matter Of Time 108
Apology Unacceptable 110
Yesterday into Tomorrow 111
In search of Cassandra...113
By a Road Side Diner 114
Touched with Paris 115
Bustng Through 117

Dedicated to Adriana, my muse, my partner

and my other half, and Cassandra, my fictitious muse,

Jena Smith, who invigorated me by giving me credit for her

nomination for the Pulitzer award in Poetry.

Looking For Madonna

Nathaniel Goldberg
AT THE CROTON DINER
© 1999

So I was lonely. Okay, I'll admit it,
I wasn't just lonely, I was terribly lonely.
At 2 in the morning I heard her
on my FM as clear as
the evening moon still eyeballing
me as I barreled down 9A toward Croton.
She had suddenly appeared inside my
radio just like that moon eye
over the Croton Harmon Station.
By two 0 two I knew it was L-O-V-E, one 2 one.
I thought of squeezing into the radio
and joining her. I began to prepare
myself for a quick entry between
the volume control and the station dial.
Should have known I couldn't fit.
By that time, Madonna had finished her song
and dissolved. I hit the train station doing
85. I expected her to be
waiting there for me on the platform.
Ah, she wasn't. At 2:15, I entered
the Croton Diner very slowly.
I didn't want to be disappointed too quickly.
Inside there was Sunny girl as radiant as ever.
Howard, Pete's son was behind the register.
Gordon sat at the counter
sipping coffee.
I walked over to Gordon real slow.
"Seen Madonna?" I asked.
"Get real," he said, and ordered two coffees.

Chaos and Kisses

Nathaniel Goldberg

She kissed me chaotically
with as much feeling as
a toad on acid
found under leaves of grass
in a pond south
of Nebraska.
Chaotic though she was
Also soft and gentle as an
evaporating memory might
or being whacked over the
the head with a mad frog leg.
Returning the favor
she bolted through
fields of wild lemmings
on their way to Kentucky
crying emptiness leaving
me sad, lost and lonely.
Together we stood yet apart,
embracing wind with our
eyes with
tear filled longings.

I saw her again in March
near the park where her
panties clung in a wind
swept by a leaf motoring
south through Illinois in
a rambunctious auto
made of scraps of
dream works.
She cried
And laughed.
"You laugh so loud
my heart burps things."
She begged me stop
"Laughter is so incestuous."

Out in Zipaquira

Nathaniel Goldberg
Last March 04-10-10

Alvaro puttered about his cave
Housed in blue light
50 Colombians,
Mostly professionals huddle in
A courtyard like birds
Winging it
Truth be known
Assembled there to partake
In a shamanistic ritual
The drinking of hooch
To enter a new consciousness
The brain dimension
Where black is blue
And blue just another color
In the night
Beware the ides of March
In the many bathrooms
As if vomitoriums in Rome
Many Latino suppers
Flew from guts
In perfect harmony
Within a dim lit profusion of
Vomiting guts

Into pastel toilets
The putrid night
Our winged passion
The solace yesterday's lunch
We saw grandpas
And grandmas
Jose killed by Para-military machetes
In breaking morning sunlight we hugged our
Distrust away,
50Colombians and one gringo Jew
Up the mountainside to
Celebrate the passing of a new day,
A new way
A bare moment
Passion asunder
I watched
They danced Tango
Fever in Zipaquira
in a palace in my mind
clinging to each other like jelly fish
I'm in Heaven
I thought.

A Hand in the Dark

A hand darkened by space full inclinations
disconnected, floats aloft like some bitten off
paralysis a floating miasma.
With thumb cocked .
as it
approached flapping
about with knuckles bending wildly
in serious nervousness.
Some rabid butterfly
flipping through the night.
A dissonant chord on life's piano,
perhaps it was malfunctioning
in an orchestra of silence,
a conductor's hand grasping
for that baton that was not there.
I spoke to the hand,
Who are you, dense hand in the night?
It only continued, fingers spreading
and grasping my throat in a grip
that was not only irresistible not
at all nice. When I tried to break

free, it Squeezed tighter till I felt
my consciousness drift
from me in abject horror.
What fiend would own such
a hand, perhaps E .A. Poe
being a conductor instead of
writer, He might use it for
such despicable means.
I charge you hand,
to be gone.
And thus I awoke
with finger marks
on my throat.
And a extreme dryness
on my pallet.

Dancing Huevos

I dream in colored
thoughts of Candelaria
Profusely locked inside me
As those seven beers it took
To undress my mind
To dance that salsa punctuality
I watched to imitate their
Angular motion
My notion another freaken beer
To clear those webs away
From my brain
So I too could do that sort of thing
In Candelaria
And finally did
To the chagrin
Of those Colombians
Who knew and watched
After my eighth Club Colombia
They pointed at my silly dancing
Yelling "Americanos"

Dancing With The Butcher's Wife

In the park with A.

Dark early morning
few pedestrians
fog spills over
the park like sheets
of dust
the world is filled with music
your image so close
through my mind.
I hear you humming
and wonder what it is
like in your country.
I walk near you listening
and remember you
young, vibrant.
When I approach
your breath is near my face
and I think of
your body
Darkness has subdued me

I stop, face you,
reach out to touch your skin
there is only
ether.
I am alone

A touch of Summer White

Last summer
In Marguerite's room near
Bleeker
In a Barrow Street alleyway,
Chumleys, an ancient speak easy
connected the past to the present.
It's raconteur memories
amidst shelves of books,
Bullfinch to Bratigan
Gave me an image
of perfection.
I dreamt her
into reality as a muse or
soul mate might manifest.
"As you like it" she might have announced
mixing Shakespeare
into a likeable cocktail.
She sniffed at me as a dog might.
Then threw herself in front of me
embellished from the universe as
bronze figurine might stand.
We left Chumleys shortly and
went to that six AM Cafe
on Bleeker near Mcdoughal to
a garden in the back near the dead tree

where poets hid
in hot summer nights.
She was
evolution waiting
to transform.

We sipped cheap wine
and discussed Chaucer and Canterbury
in a "nice to have met you" madness.
Into the twilight we burst
She provocatively haunting me.
The displeasure of pleasure way of
disappearing into the decadence of Greenwich Village.

Is it an Illusion?

Colombian Princess
Nathaniel Goldberg
07-25-09

Night life Princess
Does your laundry
What does she really think
Does she curses you beneath
Her breath?
Is she's happy
With her eight year marriage?
Or prefers another nest.

Like so many, has she become Americanized
Has she taken enough of your crap
Would prefer a different trap
Or is she afraid
To taste other possibilities?
Might she find it was better on a cool surface
Than a hot water bottle
What did she mean
An old man's love
is like a babies ass.
not strong enough to topple her wisdom
Has he failed in her eyes?
Everyone says that in Colombia!
" Does she really love you"
Or is it an illusion?

Here We Go -Many Strange Writings

Loretta's Limo

Nathaniel Goldberg
08-27-04

February midnight
brisk cold, with lamp light
on the car wreck between 2nd. and 3 rd.
a drunken metallic summation without fingers,
a non-committal indifference
a chariot waiting for its champions
to ignite it to life.
Days, months I admired the broken lump
hoping a New York City Department of what ever
would not dispose of it before my full investigation.

Young Chinese Loretta lived on the fifth floor
I on the third in a walk up
of kitchened bathtubs and
toilets in cubicals of utter despair.
Below my chariot of fancy seemed almost aware of my intension.

Conning Loretta to join me was easy.
Forcing the doors of the wreckage not.
Together, we busted them open.
We sat on glass and dust
tried to warm our bodies
against a night's bitterness
Thus we began a journey
past New York, Chicago
the moon.
Loretta sat beside me
in her Chinese way exclaimed
"You so Klazy"

Across the Night time sadness

My car ran amuck on a road
of prolific nonsense. I stood near
the roadside waiting for a metal
wagon to drive by and rescue me
from the evils of the night.
I smoked a joint by the wayside
remembering what it was like last
Autumn while waiting for the A.A.A.
To save me from the quagmire of
my broken down automobile. I
stood near a fountain of bile
crustations and quagmire
that called me deeper into the night.
Smoked two more joints
Everythings alright.

Big Mistake

Nathaniel Goldberg

Cassandra phoned
late, crying.
Her boyfriend left her.
I told her to come over.

Four AM
Soft knocking..
I opened the door,

Elfin like in the crisp dawn
Stood Cassandra,
huge eyes of brown glaze
she'd been crying.
Pushing past, could not stop her.

She sketched
A woman on
my wall with the legs of horse
and head of woman.
Said nothing.

She slipped into
my arms.
Her sobs overwhelmed me.
Be me!
she cried
Be him!

I stood
in my living room holding her
my shoulder getting
wet from her tears.

Please Don't Squeeze

A Strangest Day

Nathaniel Goldberg

09-28-05

The day was dark
an unrelenting wind
threatened to topple trees.
The route was unfamiliar.
I was to take a train into
the city. Can't recall
parking except
I was on a subway traveling
south deep into the bowels
of Manhattan. Time kept
shifting. Late for work
I stood inside
the Telephone Company
office waiting for my
assignment. It wasn't
clear whose
phone I was to fix
or where I was to go.
Time shifted again
and I was being reprimanded
for being late.
Somewhere in the
upper 70's of New York City
a ghostly stillness

took over the day paralyzing everything.
Something was missing.
I was running over
fences trying to find my way to my
car, trying to remember where I parked.
The streets were unfamiliar.
When I found my car, it
had been stripped by a gang of
kids. Everything was gone but the body
and the engine. If I could
only start the damn thing.
"Honey, honey" the sound
swept over me like the sudden
flush of a windless wave.
I turned over and found myself
in a cold sweat next to my wife.
It had been a bad dream.
Thank God

One Station Plaza

Still hear you near
yet cool yet discrete
those smooth nubile sounds
on Division Street.
Played for you
in times bitter sweet
a cutting edge perfection
the Plaza connection,

or Was it your phrasing
your harmonies blazing
your symphonic pauses
or rhapsodic clauses
that crazed in ways
you always amazed.

Needless to say
that was your way
your kind of groove
your kind of gig
in hype so profound
it dusted the ground
with choices encoded
you kind of exploded
So clear so perfect was your
timing
like a rhythmic beat
metallically rhyming.

Still see your stage
in bitter sweet light
the azure cool
the darkness polite

like notes in fog
a fractured sensation
anomalies born
inside One Station.
Incredibly smooth,
incredibly cool,
incredible sounds
you don't learn in school.
One Station Plaza
gone out of sight .
One Station Plaza
gone South for the night.

Funny You Should Say That

Nathaniel Goldberg
Or better the instant
08-02-09

Your thought or perhaps mine
The devastation of you beneath
Me clutched into September's memory
You like a leafy node
The bending of tomorrows
Dreams segway to enchantment
Hey but I know you
You are me in reverse
You are the action
Of my reaction
If I cannot have you
Rather I'd die
Unreflective or sail
About a moon beam
In such a way
Cannot you tell
For you I'd do
What no idle chatter
Could command
What can I say
What can one say
About differentiation
The is no control, in a tear drop

It's God's Fault He Created Woman

CASSANDRA

A Touch of Summer in Winter

Greenwich Village was rain wet like
early morning soot over thin streets.
Cassandra, pristine goddess
at the corner of West Fourth near
Bleeker headed into Smalls
wearing spandex with
roller-blades.
Clunking down
steps past
jazz afficionados she skated, the Village
at her heels, a crazed Aphrodite on
a crusade to disrupt the
smoke filled room where jazz zipped
the air in paraphrases.
I watched her carouse
between thin spaces locked
in by chairs and couches
on her way to nowhere fast.
She held a twelve ouncer in her left
and a cigarette butt in her right.
She collided with the
wild pianist who whimpered
like Thelonious Monk.
Everything stopped! Cassandra,
This impish child
skated until she had carved
the place into havoc.

I saw Cassandra yesterday blading
through Washington Square in
tight blue with
a purple beret capping her head. I wanted to tell her
how beautiful
she looked.
This woman
with her young body
drew everyone's attention
as she skated the empty fountain
dizzily.
Guitars echoed
past murmurings of pot smoking hippies..
Cassandra was behind me
Then in front
circling to a crescendo, around me.
I complimented her over and over
embarrassing myself.
In sudden confusion,
She almost smiled
as if each compliment was
from an older man.

Near St. Marks Place
into winter's night
a young voice behind me
kept scolding.
Cassandra, grinned
"What an ass you are"
I almost held her hands in mine. .
Tiny birds within my fingers
Nervously I almost heard
her calling me, yet her lips
made no sense.
Suddenly she bolted from me.

As she ran
a necklace of thick beads
flew past me madly.
Her tiny chest inhaled snow flakes,
her eye lids kissed the purple
beret tightly on her head.

She kept smiling
as we sat in a Cafe on Bleeker
and Mcdougal in my mind.

All I could do was watch
Cassandra disappear,
a touch of summer in winter.

Cassandra doing Washington Square again

Cassandra roller blading midnight
through Washington Square Park
past the empty fountain
Cops tell her to leave
she laughs
wild thing
presses, teases
squeezes while
echoes of the
past reverberate
in her eyes
Got a cigarette?
I give her one
she puffs
like a vicious train
Cassandra behind
me in a dizzy frenzy
circles around me
then slips
through my confusion.
her smile,
a gift to an older man.

Cassandra's Beauty Beneath

Fifteen minutes ago
the door slammed into
finality.
I was in the kitchen preparing
breakfast of
Fresh fruit, and English muffins.
I wanted to surprise her while she slept.
But now I am
alone overcome by
waves of tiredness. I
enter my tiny bedroom
to lay down imagining the sheets move,
Cassandra laughing beneath
the covers. I jump on the bed
and whack her
with the pillow while she giggles.
I looked at her face,
at her hair in ringlets, at her
pouting lips and just want
to kiss her again and again,
but restrained myself. I see
her as an impish Goddess perhaps.
Or perhaps never here to begin with.

But You Can't Beat Home

Cassandra in the Rain

I dreamt Cassandra rollerbladed in the rain
ringlets of hair over her face.
She was soaked.
Her lips blue.
She shivered.
We touched under an awning.

I held her frail body
Trying to warm her.
stop her shaking.
As her tenseness eased,
rain kept playing
a rhythm
that made my heart dance.

We stood together
without words.
Another rainy
day in my mind
in Greenwich Village.

Cassandra—Chapter two

Cassandra drove me nuts
tonight. Couldn't decide
whether it was her boyfriend
who dumped her or me.
She paced through
my cubby hole apartment
as if she were caught in a
maze. She pouted
and sobbed.
I tried holding her
she pulled away
I was the enemy.
I wanted to feel
She had turned
my world into a purple
loneliness.
Cassandra kissed my cheek
And fled as though she hadn't ever
been here.
When I rushed out to find her
She was nowhere.
Once again she left me alone.

Cassandra at Smalls

Nathaniel Goldberg
Revised 01-26-06

Cassandra, pristine goddess
at the corner of West Fourth and
Bleeker headed for Smalls,
wearing blue spandex and
roller-blades.
Clunking down steps past
jazz afficionados, skating, leaving
Greenwich Village at her heels,
a crazed Aphrodite on
a crusade to disrupt the
smoke filled room where jazz zipped
the air in paraphrases.

My eyes crossed when she caroused
between chairs and couches
on her way to nowhere fast.
Holding a twelve ounce beer in her left
a cigarette in her right,
she collided with the
wild pianist moaning
like Thelonious Monk.
Everything stopped! Cassandra,
looking the impish child
skated, carving
the place into havoc.
Turning, she laughed
tore my shirt, kissed
me and fled.

It's Hairy Down Here

Cassandra's Moon at Croton

Cassandra went out tonight to
welcome the moon
as she does every
Lunar moon, in a celebration
with Andrea, her best friend.
They mountain climb in
the darkness with flashlights
and dance naked by the river
waiting for the awesome light to transpose
them into beings of the night.
They collect themselves like
gems in a forest of glass,
hidden from the roadside by underbrush.
They stay the nighttime through
silhouetted against rocks and trees
laying down blankets on the sand
spreading fruits and delicacies
surrounded by candlelight
to enhance their ritual. When
the sun rises in the East they pack
their things
two satisfied nymphs in the new
born day.

A Day Well Spent 03-11-04

I thought of you today
and magic went through my fingers
that drive
sent me past the brink
where creativity lurks
like a hawk poised
to strike it's prey.

thoughts
curving, winding
pathways to beginnings
music
structured math equations

Blood in my veins
rose to high levels
excitement,
possibilities
edges of endless
streets and byways
where artists dwells
passion lives at the
fingertips.

I will never be a
famous poet,
but I will live each
day productively
I will remember
the past
turmoil and garage
for today I am a star
at the brink
of powerful ideas love

I Haven't Forgotten

Nathaniel Goldberg

We parted in July
07-17-09
In Bogota on a Friday
Rushing to the Airport
Carrying half my luggage
Anxious to leave
More anxious to stay
I memorized every line on your face
The punctuation indexed in each finger
Watched your amazement transform,
Mine sculpted at door steps
In cabs, in stores, in mountains
Home a nuance
No fluctuation of peace
The laughter of silence
Everyone happy
Dancing people loco
Organic bodies
Sliding past streets
Look up
See a mountain
Pretend you're not here
But at some airport locked
To a plane
On your way home, alone.

Cervasa Self Evident

In The Night

They come as shadows
crawling up the bedroom wall.
As a child they frightened
me speaking of evil ways when dark ones
crept though the house, beings without souls
who's only desire was to frighten
children, carry them away at midnight
to a place where they would be
lost forever.
They no longer frighten me.
I am used to the broken images,
the sudden light and shadowy dances
up the wall across the ceiling
disappearing as the cars pass by.

~

No weeping willows in C Park

Conceived in 1992
Central Park near Delacorte
A saxophone plays a hilltop—
a man in a grey coat
consuming dawn
tearfully
.

Why do you cry?
I wanted to ask him
They cornered him
Near cobblestone sreets
at the 86th street transverse,
slapped him in cuffs,
accused him of disturbing
the peace.

Whose peace? Certainly not mine.
Central Park is quiet again like
the Nuyorican Café at dawn
a sleeping dog
with no conscience
yesterdays newspaper filled with fools flooding
sewers of isolation

Central park lost to the confused mind
subtle, colorless, dimly lit,
an empty nub inside—out
the endless passion
of the Plaza
An Icy mist tip toeing
across cement and trees.

This early cocktail
of soliloquies and drunken nights
the rebirth of a Sax man, now a distortion
a hologram
whispering icy benevolence over pavement.

I sit on a bench nearby waiting for
his music to breathe across my face
sweep the park.
dust darkness from my soul

Instead my feet draw butterflies
in the snow.

Passion in Central Park is gone
certainly no more weeping willows!

My Father Is

I see him standing, a tree with a patch of
white where the bark has peeled away.
There is a smoothness like an ocean
I see him connected to the earth,
a pale grey in a foggy night.
He stands above me
the tree who is my father
I feel him in the center of my neck
where the summer has gone into fall.
His beard, a painful
stubble where memory is
sand upon which I lie while
he bore me from a chest of silence.
I see around him
the many colors of tomorrows
as halos of reddish green light.
He is my memory of today
where wisps of smokey sand
pass through my stomach
through the energy of light
into a tunnel.
He is remorse
a total sorrow.
He is a willow
wearing glasses for buds
and sadness as eternal as a
bending prayer.
He is my solitude.

Papadise Is Just A Kiss Away

Senasqua

I promised my kids
a perfect sunset.
I took them down
to Senasqua at 8.
The sun like some
cataract covered eye ball
kept shifting and rolling
behind the clouds.
No scarlet streamers coursed
the veins of sky.
No blue slashes and bubbling reds,
pinks, and golds.
I looked at my son
and apologized for the
promise I couldn't keep.
My daughter laughed,
I cried.

-Nathaniel Goldberg-

What love tastes of

Nathaniel Goldberg

10-08-08
Red summer splashes
06-12-09
tears of
unbearable speed
the lose across chastity
or her yearning to taste

disappointment
trying those cobble
streets she used to wander

or is memory
thought
carved in wood like a
fixation

Does it end
or does it swallow dark
buds like summer nights
Is it a twenty four seven
bridesmaid
with severance pay.

Does it matter
does summer matter
Is it that street she lived on
bathed in winter snow a light
of cold, very cold
Does she taste of ice
Or just tears melting.

Summer Snow

1 Nathaniel Goldberg
04-30-04

Collecting shells at summer's edge
a winter's wish
to hibernate
or taste a kiss of impish smiles
on frozen lips
and heated dreams
on rays of light
as if in jest
lit up the snow
in symmetry
holding fast
among the rocks
where once I stood
collecting shells at summer's
edge to fondle each
upon a ledge of thought
where once I caught
the summer snow

Midnight Dansin

A Tree'less Orchid

Picked an orchid in my dreams
Wasn't real so it seems

Added meaning to my life
This flower stood
Inside of me
An awesome night you see
A tree of orchids so unreal
Never wrong yet might congeal instead
Not here not there
Not anywhere

This budding light of violet
Blue
A light so pure and petal soft
It summoned me
To dreams aloft
To brighten in a darkened pit
Where nightmares lay to lack of wit

Like walnut cracks inside a door
That holds a tree of flowering
Colors orchids don't grow in
Trees, for Christ sake!

Upon my knees
In my dreams alone and not so dark
Purest colors within a park
Hold fast this scene Autumnal Fall
As season's quicken within a call

To remember dreams like sudden rains
Spread rivulets across my window panes
Not meaning hurt
Nor deluge either
My sensitive friend
There's no forgiveness in

A liars oath so it seems
Or bitter end
For Christ Sake

To baron ideas an orchid on a tree indeed
So far from life and time may seed
This time and space remembrance per chance
As Oscar Wild within a dance
I'm sure never happened
Never would never should
Never could

Dance this floral disarray
In under pants they might say
Can or will not go your way
In other places you might stay
where I say slay away
or

That purple dream that gay romance
Where yes
I wore no under pants
Never do never will
So watch my orchid,
Let it chill.

You no time for me
I no time for you,
Tis true

Perhaps we grow does pain remain,
Orchids too do grow in Spain.
Not on trees indeed

A Bottle Of Wine

Nathaniel Goldberg

1:40 AM 02-22-03
Bought a 15 dollar bottle of wine
sure was fine, a divine wine,
red ros/e, hey hey, that's what I say,
drank that bottle down to the throttle
one two three, jiffy ooh we
whoa was me
sat on the floor, drank me some more
ma head was swimmin and I was brimmmin
with lips a trimmin
down to the very last drop
with one very cool pop
twas dry oh my, how high was I
opened ma mouth
closed my eyes
ma lips was numb, laughed till I cried
oh my oh my oh my oh my
how cool was I, so high,
oh my oh my, lips were dry
I was high,
oh my laughed til I cried
Oh my.
Loved that feel
the real deal
feather weather
wine and tether
like a pillow willow
inside some heather.
Now I'm drunk like a skunk
Oh my, oh my, oh my.
Never ever want to die
just fly and fly into the sky
keep it cool, keep it high
oh My oh my oh my oh my.

Finding You

Nathaniel Goldberg

I can't stop thinking of you
Colombia, the flesh of night 08-0
Toned with green eyes
A smile that does not end

Today is your birthday
I see you as I drive
The many towns
Among
tiny secrets
a jewelry store
hidden in marble
and Latino dreams
an insignificant store
of glass cases and
stone carved thoughts
encased remembrances
Expensive necklaces
I found you
Of peridot teardrops
to match your eyes

Ah Heck

Shakespeare and Co.

We met George Whitman on a foggy Monday in Paris
The old man had charm, wit
and the bite of viper
His bookstore, *Shakespeare and Co.*
faced the Seine across from Notre Dame
He gave us free lodging
in his Tumbleweed hotel/bookstore
three old floors warped with
the weight of old Paris
where famous writers passed through
slept in uncomfortable beds
left their signatures
under the rickety counter
amidst dusty books
The gifted young soul's
smooth words mingled
among cracked bindings
No wonder George gets younger
in his prolific garden.

I suppose that's one way of looking
at a poem. Not mine.
eyes stuffy, ostentatious
not my Paris.
as is often the case with retouched poems.

What can one say about lost sensibility
that interruption breeds distraction
George Whitman was forgotten way beyond such possibilities
in his garden of Proustian, Joycean Oxford girls who dotting
his book store with many periods
deck upon deck, floor upon floor
novels being sold by handsome young ladies
to pay for their stay at the Shakespear and Company Hotel
perky intelligencia causing his heart
to rise like the fountain in front of the bookstore
which peed perpendicular.

The invite was nice
Thank you George
sleep in his hotel amidst misty maidens
I thought, we thought,
however after closer inspection the bed bugs
dissuaded us. Roaches bed bugs who knew
what else in this Henry Miller
paradise of Paris perpendicular

Instead of staying we invited George, Marie Parisian hater of
Parisians
Steve and myself coupled with three bottles of bad wine
to a cave
of a restaurant somewhere on

the left bank where gold noses
sniffed bullion out of the pockets
of unsuspecting fools.
The only thing worse than the wine was the steak
It tasted like rubberized feet,
and smelled just as bad.
George was cheap
What can I say,
Being around profound wisdom
must suck at one's purse strings serrupticiously
but then Paris was full of sounds
The rickety cobbled streets
embedded with darkness
and jazz as if one was
tantamount to the other
Nights flaked with subterranean
passage, a willowed shell housing
not only passion but the morning whispers
where bakers began their creative tedium
birthing bagettes.
Paris dear Paris perfumed eyes inside the Pompidou
The Louvre so young a visioned beauty
your pretentious monolithic pyramid leading
you like a dog
and there you are Jim Morison

buried beneath near that bridge
just beyond vision, making an awkwardly
placed tomb so most might
leave you rest.
Now even your star studded city
your profanity of lights has become a cliché.
Well Paris, adieu, I bid you farewell.
I probably will never see you again
I will miss you even though I hate you,
you ambivalent state of existential nausea.
I love your woman, hate your subway system, your busses
your fluff of phony nostalgia. What really bugs me is
where you burned Joan of Ark, You built a Mcdonalds.
Nearby.

Village Underground

We ran Greenwich Village ragged
two perplexed drunkards
hitting on girls in manic delirium
smashed to bits on rot gut wine
and Benzedrine chasers

Third Avenue—the Bowery
Holy Motherfucker
They were there, our kin within
the philosophical, the editorial
the benidictarians all piss drunk
Research was defunct.
No Allen Ginsberg fornicating
or pontificating about his love for Peter Orloffsky.
No Zimmerman's cornering illusions
with a bending voice and a broken guitar.
Instead here they were, The Magical Mystery
ragimuffins blessed with abject knighlihood
the goon platoon around the corner from the
Dom, the palisades of witticism
Christianity circumcised
beards of infected manifestations
and no one cared.
Frankly Kerouac I don't give a damn!!

Go North young man
a Connecticut dream
where the Bowerys lost
or so it might seem
the peripheral's gone
there's music here
but fancy this the sound sucks, my dear

A Bare Room

poetic fever
Nathaniel Goldberg
01.15.10

I possess
A room bare of feeling
A place to hide
From a barnacled past
Without anyone's crap
Sitting in a corner
Like an
Empty wine bottle
Contemplating
Anger, disillusionment
Stupidity
Busting into my life
Like wet toilet paper.
Even though they exist
Neither here nor there
Let them sink in a quagmire
Of their own misguided nonsense

Who Gave That Kid A Club Columbia

Around The Rainbow— Jazz Po 06-17-01 Dr. Hawk

Nathaniel Goldberg

Around the rainbow I road 21 Hillcrest Ave.
spoke to no one Crotonville NY
couldn't care less 10562
broke a glass of wine (914) 923-4006
across a fine line (845) 222-0019
of here nor there
not anywhere
Saw a thousand colors
worriers and brothers
couldn't control
my bitter ness
flooded with glass across
my chest
had no rest
had no test
could not contest
the virgin ness
of September's rain
insane rain
rainbow rain
across my window pain
damn Sam
couldn't land a jam
cutting over and under
and through and around
beneath the rainbow
there is no sound
only the sound of the ground
beneath my feet
could have been neat
but never cried before
never lied before, never died before. Had to hide before. Yeah

A Wind Chilled Day In New York

Nathaniel Goldberg

12-19-05

Clinging to a lamp post
for salvation
thinking of you
in Bogota
no snow or
dreadful gusts.
You are warm
secure
in your Colombia.
Here December
grazes 20 degrees.
My coat is heavy,
your coat light.
It never gets
cold in Bogota.
New York
gets bone cold.
When I see you
on February
eleventh
I will hold you
and realize that our
relationship is more
than one sided.
I wait for you in
my dreams.
There are
so many variables.
Will the airport be
closed due to inclement
weather.
No matter.
I will be with you
Soon.

A Night to Her

A night next to her is like a shoe without a foot.
But what can one say about feet.
Shoeless perhaps on a rocky road
or connoting helplessness
walking in a cloudless night
unclothed but for one breast in the middle of a chest
in a night of fog and chewing gum drawers
Could one feel shoeless while
strapped to a canoe-less
dream, footed to a pedal—less bicycle
or how does one pontificate in a negative
state of nebular conundrum.?

What the hell can one tell about one foot from a naked tit?

Yeah

But Pure Infinity

The ocean, bluish green glass eyes
like her eyes.
Wooden boats sway
beyond windy trees.

Below puffy clouds
A hawk gliding through violet light
sets on a rooftop
to wait..

Where are the blackbirds
that never sleep
living on decaying carcasses
of road kills.

Today there is no warmth
in the ocean
Yet still, the poised hawk
a garden of night kills
now smooth
where passion
is a bending eyelid
a Dali painting

There is no taste
nor sleep but pure infinity.

The Night Before

Nathaniel Goldberg

24 Amalfi Drive
Sunday morning madness Cortlandt Manor NY 10567
Saturday night's heat still in the sheets 8 July 2000
Sunshine blasting through the windows Jan.9 2006
like happiness

Last evenings' shadows gone
I rise through streams of light
fog over the bathroom mirror
distorts my vision
the residue of sleep in my eyes

Dancing through the mist of my shower
droplets along her skin
she emerges into memory
a wet ivory carving

The dream busting into Sunday
dancing over
cold tiles
radiant hair hanging over
her tiny breasts like rain

She is a ravishing amethyst

She is Cassandra
from the night before

What I need most

Nathaniel Goldberg

06-10-09
That taste in your eyes
When they smile
The cross section your thighs
Land slide pushing your lipstick
Paradise over your mouth
Connecticut fingers that dance
Over my body like skating nails
To you I pretend you descend
Into me sixteen inches beyond
Kentucky where March pretends
Spring descends
Though care might share
That man—woman devastation
Blood on ice
Thrown twice
Into clogged thievery
Terminally
when you came through me.

Stone Cole Mama

ADRIANA

Adriana's Magic

Nathaniel Goldberg
09-15-05

Adriana learns to drive.
I sort of relax
in the passenger seat.
With my hands between my legs
And my heart stuck under my foot.
Cars lined up for miles
in the opposite direction.
Lucky Adri.
If traffic were the other way she
Would be late.
Her life winds and twists
In an astounding metaphor
She scholarshiped her way through
School, from Colombia
Into my New York social life
Some extraordinary happening
Bursting my life
Into my wife
With her potion
Dynamite mixed with
Fixations; obstinate
Refracted,
One hell of a magic
Show.

The pain of death within

I saw you last night in a dream
while you slept in my arms
I felt your breath against my neck
looked at your face in the faint blue light
saw the smile on your lips
tasted the salt of tears down my face

heard your heart in my mind like
a thumping deep inside my brain
wanted to awaken you so I could
tell you again and again how I
missed you yesterday and the
day before and the day before that

Don't recall what you said to me
in my dream
except you were completely irascible
like an oncoming train
in a silent night
rushing through my thoughts

heard the pat of your belly
against mine in a song that was
despair while we made love.
They had taken you away from
me muñeca
Sent you back to Columbia

I die every moment,
but love the pain of remorse
a tiger in a pit of my stomach
Biting me to death.

A Walk with My Lady

Nathaniel Goldberg

24 Amalfi Drive
Every day we walk along Amalfi Drive Cortlandt Manor
I notice something new, New York 10567
the pond beyond the hill, the fallen spruce Tel (914) 736-5542
from old age and many storms..
I wonder how long
this towering Olympus
swayed in winds
till its ancient
arms broke from its own weight?
its leafless, weak branches
must have suffered till its finality.
Other things touched me
like the sculptured image of
liquid glass, the pond I
never noticed rushing down the way
behind thirty four Amalfi Drive.
Or the newborn rose deciding to blossom
waiting for its owner
to break off its stem
as if its beauty missed.
And the sky always new with
mythical change, its calming grace
as if to collide within itself
so I and my lady
can watch its darkening turmoil of
strata cumulus threatening rain
in a beauty of imaginations.
It's so good to be alive.

How Big Can A Foot Get

Next To My Lady

This morning
during a jazz riff
over W.B.G.O.
she sleeps in my arms
her silken flesh against me
the soft flow of her breath
against my shoulder.

Outside the sun begins to rise
the trees designing the background.

Four chairs relaxed around
our wooden table balanced
poetically
the folded umbrella centered
elegantly.

a sculptured painting
out on the lawn.

Here on Amalfi Drive
it is so different from
what I am used to.
No traffic din.

I turn off the radio
She remains beside me in
the profuse silence
of a blissful morning.
Thus, my life begins again.

I'm Not With Her Now

I'm not with her now,
Oh, I miss her.
We were together so long
she became part of me.

She wanted to work
to be productive.
We were financially inept
but it didn't
matter because money was secondary.
As long as the rent got paid
and we were able to eat.

I miss the gentleness of her voice,
her incredibly subtle accent.
I miss the sharpness of her mind,
I miss her sitting outside on
our deck at the table next to my window
while she studied English.
She always wore those incredibly sexy sun glasses
with the wide lenses.
Her bare legs propped by a chair.
She kept the table's umbrella down
so she could bathe under the hot sun.

When I'd see her at nine thirty after work
she'd run to my arms.
There were no
barriers for emotions.
No guidelines for passion
Only the weight of thinking.

Perhaps we saw too much of each other
or went to the Croton Diner too often,
or those momentary sojourns
to the Black Cow, the local coffee house.

My band and I did a gig the other night in Peekskill.
She was sitting in the corner sipping a glass
of wine
listening to me sing.
I kept my eyes
closed envisioning her
like a snapshot.
I saw her black blouse
against the back drop of a white wall
like the silhouette of a painting.

When I opened my eyes she was
gone.

You and Me at the A and P

Tonight, I couldn't't help myself
in the isles of the A and P
I grabbed my wife, Adri,
held her tight against me,
grasped her, kissed her
felt her pulse in her chest
with one great big caress
no one saw us

I didn't care anyway,
you see it was my day,
like every day, like I always say,
Today is my day.
We just stood there in the isle
near the squash and tomatoes,
the onions and potatoes,
the radishes as big as Gladiolas

We just stood there kissing
like it was a whim we were missing,
when if fact we always kiss,
as though it was the first time,
like the first rhyme,
like every night she drives me wild,
my angle being, my God sent child.

What Beauty Hath Devoured My Mind

You Balance My Lopsided World

Darling, you came to me
last night
in a dream that transposed my sanity.

You were smiling
as you so often do in dreams.
I kissed you softly
as you slept
only to awaken you
as I often do these nights
to make sure you are real.

After all you are my sanity
within this insane world.

It seems we've been together for
infinity,
when in reality it's only been eleven months.
You, who counterbalance my outer weights
like Borders Books after they threw me out
just the year before we met.

You ease the pain,
take away the bitterness.
Touch upon sensibility
destroy all ugliness
patch the holes in my universe

Yes, you balance my lopsided world.

Deja Vous

Yesterday I had that feeling
we met before,
especially when we're close.

Events fly through my mind like ravens.
You told me you had the same sensation.
Every time we're close
things come back to me.
There was a beach of black sand.
the coral sea
matched your eyes.
You said it was Santamarta
in your country.
You said you remembered my long hair
That we had met on that beach many
years before.
That you were little and your hair
was in pig tails.
I was much younger.
You were building a sand castle.
I tripped and broke its turret.
You cried and I held you in my arms.
You were young, but so was I.
I told you we'd meet again some where
And here you are my wife.

Ginsberg

I saw Ginsberg last night in a dream,
he kept poking his fucking finger in my face.
Like it was a finger of humility.
His hairy snake arm
hung over Whiteman's
shoulder.

Kerouac was there, you bet cha,
standing on some street corner
smoking a joint.

Even Ferlinghetti was there from California
fornicating a hole in a copy of his City Lights obituary.
His epitaph: written by himself. "Death to me is like a sea of
urination." He waited all these years to pontificate his last
hurrah.
Oh heated year, Whitman's queer
a sucker for nonessential Bullshit
Oh dear, oh dear Oh dear.

Dylan passed by with a bible
of Christianity spilling
Jewdaism from his game;
Jesus on the run.
Only Whiteman, I presume had earlier
passed on now to the other side
Saw the other passing by me
Kerouac.
The white bearded Whitman, friend
Kerouac, compulsive Burroughs.
Dear Peter, I said in tears

Allen must be in heaven by now.
Does he still make verse colliding
with other heavens or did the saints
still his voice for
eternity? He told me Warhol was miss-diagnosed.
They killed the poor sucker.
Bob Dylan used to sing on Bleeker
off Sixth, his guitar case collecting
coins from his audience. Now
it collects dust in a corner. There's
no more Beat Generation.
The days of the Hippies are gone forever
I watched them trickle by, saw
them paraded in front of me
like toy soldiers on a table
in my dream as if postings from the past.
I saw them in Greenwich Village, Haight Ashberry
even in Paris.
They came to my funeral like hawks circling
to bring me home.
They told me of love and abandonment.
I saw Marguerite Young in her grave.
Everyone was there.

And Then There Were Two

Metro Politan Madness

Nathan Hawk

Why? Or what roulette madness
47th between Lex. and Third
Two wheeling thunder
Motorcycle madness
A well oiled dream
Turmoil in a sliver night
Butterfly speed
High as high gets
Panama Red
Unbeatable,
The crutch of human
Dilemma
Dilemma time
60, 70 85 on a city street
Closing in
The corner
Coming at me in night
Turned destructive
The banter of derision
Derisive temptation
Like witches hanging from street lamps
Like swinging wagons didn't they?
What difference
What about the badness of perception
Perhaps the gallant Che or Castro
Or Steve Wonder or Blind Lemon

These souls who prefer not t see
The darkness about them
Waves of thunderous destruction
They are clear now
These empathetic monuments
In heightened worlds
But I
A child from of violent nature
Chose perfection in escape
85 in a thirty
I bet if Jesus had a bike with
A high powered engine
He would have done
Similar
Or was it the ability to see
Light in a darkened turbulence?

Paris You're Jewish

I know,
I am, also.

You're a bad ass
with excessive spass
enough to burn the pants off
any bitch
under which
you might consider
crass
a trait, irate
that suits you too.

In truth
Collectively
we think alike
wild, child mind
an uncontrollable passionate
spike
passion
for sure.

Doesn't deserve jail
the quaintly quail
has only to
launch her,
like a Martha
Stewart springboard
beyond fame into stardom

Alas, Paris, indeed
You're very cool
you rule with
insatiable need
a bitter school
life above the burbs
where funds control
a saddened blast
parading past
the pole of negative
fusion .

You deserve
fame with pain
because you are
one hell of a wealthy
non-conformist inane
in your own way
I suppose
Or one might say
Insane.

The Music Gone

It is soft
everything still
the world slumbers in quietude

There is no music
save the hum of my computer
Adriana sleeps in the next room

TV voices drone through mid-night
She sneezes as Letterman pontificates
Somber blue light glowing
from my ancient computer

It's as though it wants to dance
If it had feet it would leap
from its moorings across
the living room laughing

Imagine a dancing computer
Maybe I am being spooked
by my electronic living room

I already miss today's love fest
leaping past folds
pure peace

I live for these times

To please you, to tease you
to ease you, to squeeze you
You are. You just are.

And Then, Then Three

September In Paris

A brisk wind blew over
the narrow cobble stone street
Down below we heard
the sturdy sound of a trumpet
playing to the dawn
raising the dead
the many Morrison 's
in their Parisian graves
We threw money from our balconies
As did others until
this rambunctious man with
His rambunctious horn
turned it off and went away.
Paris was awakened on the
Wrong side of the bed.

What actually killed Papa? 07-16-08

Was it suicidal dogma
the prolific sound of
the shot gun blast resonating the walls
blowing his literary brains
to smithereens or was it
shock treatments,
destroying his memories
his abilities to write

perhaps it was the Mayo's Clinic's
experimentation with ECT (electro convulsive therapy?)
That blew apart Hemingway's
world leaving him lost
to the remembrances of things past

Ernest was ailing, sure, depressed yes,
but they killed him, not the shotgun.
like Andy Warhol and Truman Capote at
New York Hospital, the pit of the NY pendulum
The true madness is in a world of madness,
it lies in modern medicine.
What can one say of Hemingway?
That he lost him memory, then his sensibility?
Alas poor Ernest.

NEWS BRIEF:

In the late fifties, the Hemingways moved from Cuba to Ketchum, Idaho so Ernest could hopefully recover from his deteriorating health. He wrote A Moveable Feast, his memoirs. He checked twice into the Mayo Clinic to be treated for his physical ailments as well as depression, but was not helped much. He began receiving shock treatment but, as Meyers writes, Aone of the sad side effects of shock therapy is the loss of memory, and for Hemingway it was a catastrophic loss. Without his memory he could no longer write, could no longer recall the facts and images he required to create his art@ (205). Having lost his ability to write and still ailing physically, he lost the will to live. On July 2, 1961, three weeks before his 62nd birthday, Hemingway shot himself in the head with a shotgun.

Ode To A Shell

A shell tucked
in my hand
like a tiny bird

What do you know
of awkward dreams?
Or perhaps you do—
more than I

Perhaps you suffer
eternal damnation
or your hardness is
nearly as corrupt
as mine

Dear shell
did you house
a mollusk

Did you protect
as I once did
in my first marriage

Did that small
insignificant being
that hid inside you
burst forth to
find
another shell
another poem.

Once I Dreampt Upon A Star

A Matter Of Time

Nathaniel Goldberg
01-31-07

Six years
of suspended time
like finding a lost Renoir

Six years
of glazed touches
devilish intentions

Jealous thoughts
colliding thoughts
imprudent thoughts

coming together
falling
arms flailing
I remember
December when we married

a cold winter night in Manhattan
She didn't know me
She didn't know me
She didn't know me

She, from Colombia
painted my life
with feathers and

Latin promises
The dust of forgiveness
Brilliance of mind

playing yesterday
orchestrating seconds
not trusting

But last night she said

"I've fallen in love with you."

Apology Unacceptable

April 1 2009
Nathaniel Goldberg

Why did I apologize for your perception?
You Perhaps as uneducated as a turkey's rectum
why didn't I stand up to your pompous lack
of manners, your disillusionments which
brought you here in the first place?

You are not just a lonely person,
but a female Donna kejote
calculating like a knife blade piercing
a bodiless carcass
to poke to dislodge to rearrange

Show me what I have shown you
and gladly would I
jump into a tub of glue
If not, stick a lump of sourdough
up your rectal mind
because true education is hard to find.

Yesterday into Tomorrow

Awoke at four AM with the taste of
morning in my mouth.
She was gone or perhaps
was never here.
Poured cereal
into my blue delft
bowl with my name on it.
Watched milk lift kernels
each one a world
within itself.
Thought about her
in the morning haze.
Cassandra, myth,
figment of my imagination,
joining me in early morning hours
to haunt me
drive me mad.
Her face a shadow
against the whiteness of
a winter morning, the coldness
of a glassy day.
The sum of all seasons
yesterday into tomorrow.

And Then

In search of Cassandra

I went to Paris last week
in search of Cassandra.
I looked
behind pillars and
monuments went to the museums
where the tourists hung out
even Shakespeare and Co.
where the angels gathered.
Ah, she wasn't there. She might have
been the young blond, Pia or the lovely
Hanna. I went to the Champs de lisee
walked for miles, approaching strangers
for no apparent reason. Paris was cold
and unfriendly. The Musee Picasso,
The Dorcee the Louvre but none held
the perfect one or perhaps she doesn't exist.

By a Road Side Diner

Texas looms.
Short skirted oil-wells
flat land, dust
freckled faced
priceless—child
sunset eyes
morning child
devouring days with
breathless charm
tiny hands
sweet voiced anger
turning Amarillo
by drawing Bush
over the internet
with daggers through
his heart

brought the secret service
to her parents
threatening to send
her to Juvenile hall.

Where do we live?

Touched with Paris

Soft, sedate dipped in hell
strapped to a table
where lonely ladies
sipped wine in a frosty atmosphere
no wisdom
no thunder
only Paulette
yesterday before yesterday
screwed to the bed posts like
a handcuffed rooster
a french bouquet
in West Bank Soot
I met her, uncovered
her and plastered her by the
the Seine
near Morrison's
grave
he
might have been
lost
this way that way
anyway
Paulette, Parisian epitome
dancing on glass
in her under things
a crazy fixation
chasing every heart
in Paris.
Would never happen in New York

I Hope It Never Stops

Bustng Through

Nathaniel Goldberg

Flew to Bogota Friday 07-15-09
The weight of New York
Lifted like a monetary fog
As I recall
Bogota coolness
Replaced
No Hudson romance
Or village dance
But Colombian beauty marking
Hill sides drawn to
Hey love, call me a cab
Friday night busting through
Salsa
La gente
T he world purified past
The bite
Of yesterday's fear, have a beer
She stood wearing a ruana
Like Eastwood in a spaghetti western
Or the warmth of Santa Marta
Artistically supersized
Like the midnight streets
Of Bogota sheathed in romance
Of More beer no care